CW00392291

The Steaming Sixties

Stirring episodes from the last decade of Steam on BR

1. A North East Redoubt
by Paul Anderson

ISBN-10 1-903266-99-8
ISBN-13 978-1-903266-99-1
First published in 2008 by Irwell Press Ltd., 59A, High Street, Clophill, Bedfordshire, MK45 4BE
Printed by KONWAY PRESS.

They were scruffy, typified a dying era and were about to close when most of the photographs in this book were taken, but the sheds at Tyne Dock, Blyth, West Hartlepool and Sunderland had a definite charm about them, of not-too genteel decay. They housed the remaining BR steam locomotives employed on moving mineral traffic in County Durham and Northumberland, a pedigree stretching back over a century and a half. Furthermore, some of the mainly unkempt engines allocated to the four sheds in their last year had experienced very interesting careers.

Locos still active in the North East during 1967 included two venerable and robust North Eastern Railway designs, the P3 0-6-0s (later J27) and T2 0-8-0s (later Q6). The other surviving engine of North Eastern design was a J72 0-6-0T, this particular example having been built by BR. There were three other types of main line locomotives in the North East. These were the War Department 2-8-0 'Austerities', originally meant to last just two years, the K1 2-6-0s, of LNER design but built after Nationalisation and the Ivatt 2-6-0s of LMS origin, but mainly built by BR. Fortunately there is one of each of the above classes preserved.

The author wishes to acknowledge the information provided by the RCTS 'Green Books' and *Railways of Consett and North West Durham* by G. Whittle (David & Charles 1971). Of use too was Ian Sixsmith's episode 7 in his series of articles *North Eastern Locomotive Sheds* in *British Railways Illustrated* Vol.16 No.9, June 2007: *Tyne Dock: 'A Tripe Supper with leftover monies'*. I am also grateful to Pip Bloor for shed allocations, Paul Roberts for loco details from the Internet, Frank King for Shed Directory information and Bryan Wilson (via Irwell Press) for notes on signalling. Fred and John Holyoak, Dave Wells, Malc Deacon and Steve Hoskins also provided help. Special thanks also to Phil Hoskins for IT rescue efforts and Sharon Barnes for typing some of it so quickly.
Paul Anderson, Leicester 2008.

Cover photograph. **See page 25**

Opposite. **Although Q6 63429 at Tyne Dock shed on Tuesday 21 March 1967 typifies the run-down of steam, there was a certain dignity about these fine engines at the end of their lives. The distinctive outline includes a capuchon or 'windjabber', as the North Eastern preferred to call the lip on the chimney. Photograph A.G. Forsyth, Initial Photographics.**

A fine industrial panorama looking directly north from Tyne Dock Bank Top signal box on the morning of 21March 1967. The River Tyne is running north-eastwards at this point and North Shields forms the hazy skyline to the left, while the outskirts of South Shields occupy the right background. Bank Top cabin derived its name from the double track route running through the centre of this view, the climb from the quays to the box being around 60 feet. Wagons occupying the middle distance are in Tyne Dock Yard. The miscellaneous sidings on the left will be described later. WD 2-8-0 90370 has probably just been coaled and is heading for the 'main line' from Tyne Dock Bottom. The engine has a 56A Wakefield shed plate and that depot's name on its buffer beam. However, it was definitely allocated to Tyne Dock in May 1967 and was withdrawn from Sunderland later that month. Towards the end there was little enthusiasm for changing shedplates. Prior to its move to the North East the Austerity had spent its entire BR career at Wakefield. Photograph A.G. Forsyth, Initial Photographics.

In early morning sunshine on 23 March 1967, Q6 63387 shunts in Tyne Dock Yard. The line from Tyne Dock Bottom to Bank Top is away to the left while the North Shields skyline peers above rakes of mineral wagons. Some of the roads in this yard led to four stone coal-loading jetties at the head of the basin. Tyne Dock had a long history. The Stanhope & Tyne Railroad opened to South Shields in 1834 and the eastern section became the Pontop & Jarrow in 1842. These concerns actually considered building additional staithes at the site where Tyne Dock was eventually constructed, but nothing happened until the North Eastern was formed in 1854. Work began in 1855 and the impressive 50 acre basin opened in March 1859. 63387 was completed at Darlington Works in November 1917, the only one delivered that month. It was withdrawn from West Hartlepool shed in September 1967, having been observed on trips to Tees Yard and Thornley Colliery, among other places, during the last days of BR steam in the North East. Photograph A.G. Forsyth, Initial Photographics.

This is Tyne Dock Bank Top signal box looking north during the early afternoon of 9 August 1968. The brick building to the left of the cabin is described on an LNER plan as 'Power House' and the wooden shed to the left of that as the 'Trains Office'. Rails on the left led to Tyne Dock shed (behind the camera) while the line from Tyne Dock Bottom climbs from the centre of the view. Beyond the retaining wall and bank to the right is Tyne Dock Yard. Metal railings this side of the signal box surround a cutting and tunnel mouth where the North Eastern Pelaw-Jarrow-Tyne Dock line of 1872 (now part of the Tyne & Wear Metro) passed beneath the Tyne Dock complex. Immediately to the right of the box is a two-signal post, with one of the arms raised for the engine shed roads. The other controlled a link to the 'main line' from Tyne Dock Bottom. Facing signals on the impressive signal bridge, right to left, are as follows. Prominent in the centre is the down main for Dock Bottom, then comes the removed board for Standage Line 1, the surviving board for Standage Line 2, a little post for 'Inward Engine Line', the missing signal for the Coal Stage and a tiny signal for 'Gantry'. These terms will be explained in a later view. Photograph A.G. Forsyth, Initial Photographics.

Looking south into mid-day sunshine on 21 March 1967. This shows Tyne Dock Bank Top box, the line to Green Lane on the left and Tyne Dock shed in the middle distance. A couple of locos simmer on the road to 'No.1' roundhouse, while Green Lane box on its gantry above the tracks can be seen in the distance to the left of the shed. The furthest-left facing signals on the bridge comprise Bank Top's up main Starter, with Green Lane's Distant below it. To the right of it is the down main to up main lead, then the down main-wagon shops lead. This was a significant railway site some time before the engine shed and Tyne Dock itself were established. Lines to the left of the shed marked the course of the Brandling Junction Railway's Brockley Whins-Green Lane-South Shields line of 1839, paralleled by the Stanhope & Tyne Railroad of 1834. Beyond the box, the railings again mark the course of the 1872 Jarrow line. The signalman peers out of his box; more of him overleaf. Photograph A.G. Forsyth, Initial Photographics.

A study in concentration at Tyne Dock Bank Top box on 21 March 1967. The cabin dated from 1902 and was re-framed in 1937. Of the 35 levers, 29 were working. Levers in this view were painted red for home signals, yellow for distants, black for points and white for out of use. Other colours (not shown here) were brown for releasing a ground signal so that it could be operated from track level, blue for locking facing points and black and white chevrons for detonator placers. The signalman, cloth in hand to keep the lever handle free of condensation, is releasing No.14, having already released the lead (point) lever No.16. Note that the signal lever has 16 on the side indicating that the lead must always be pulled first. Nos.14 and 16 let a loco out of the coaler road so that it could access the 'main line' and watering facilities. On the block shelf above the levers, from right to left, were the Block Bell with the Tapper below it to send a signal to Tyne Dock Bottom, the Line Clear/Occupied Indicator and the Signal Repeater. The last-named is related to the levers in the far corner, No.1 being Tyne Dock Bank Top's Home Signal; No.2 is Bank Top's Starter on the signal bridge outside and No.3 the box's Distant well away to the left. This was the order in which signals were cleared for a train from Tyne Dock Bottom. The Signal Repeater showed if the Distant signal was fully pulled off. Photograph A.G. Forsyth, Initial Photographics.

A rather superfluous signal at the throat of Tyne Dock Yard on 9 August 1968, the lines it once controlled having been disused for some time. This is clearly an 'economical' North Eastern signal with arms for both directions and a lightweight lattice post, although the almost oriental finial is rather nice. Bank Top box is away to the left, behind the camera, while the Newcastle-Jarrow-South Shields passenger line, having tunnelled under the yard approach, is away to the right at a lower level beyond the retaining walls, but this side of the hopper wagons. The factory with the tall chimney is a biscuit and cake works in Rutland Street off Boldon Lane, West Harton. A couple of signals in the left middle distance are featured on the next few pages in happier times. Photograph A.G. Forsyth, Initial Photographics.

Looking north in morning sunshine, this view shows Q6 63387 pottering around the approach to the second of four (from the west) fans of sidings at Tyne Dock Yard on 23 March 1967. Bank Top box is 300 yards away to the left and behind the camera. Note the complex nature of the site, which has been crafted out of a slope down to the river and includes banks, mounds and cuttings between the flat ground required for the tracks. There is a hint of the North Shields skyline, but the foreground and middle distance is dominated by at least 36 telegraph poles, many of which double up as yard lighting posts. Furthermore, a couple of brick cabins associated with shunting the yard add to the interest. Completing the scene are four rather fine North Eastern signals which feature in detail on the next few pages. Photograph A.G. Forsyth, Initial Photographics.

A close-up of the right side of the view opposite, on the same day. This small fragment of the immensely complex layout at Tyne Dock Yard reveals the throat of the third fan of sidings to the right of the cabin, followed by a snaking ascent to the easternmost and fourth set of sidings. A miniature forest of ground point levers is in evidence, and note the well-manicured ballast even at this late date. Mineral wagons of several generations can be seen to the left and a brake van is perched at a higher level to the right of the cabin, typical of the almost unfathomable layout. In the right background are some of the 32 Victorian dwellings in the appropriately-named cul-de-sac Station Cottages, on the other side of Boldon Lane from Tyne Dock station. The roof of the large building left of them belongs to the Picture Palace cinema. Photograph A.G. Forsyth, Initial Photographics.

This once-proud but rather dilapidated North Eastern signal at the approach to the second fan of sidings was seen a couple of views earlier, although it did seem to be happily functioning then, showing a lower-quadrant aspect and maybe helping 63387 perform its duties on the same day, 23 March 1967. The finial has been removed and the top capped. There is an operating number 2 on the post, just above its black base. Industry on the north bank of the Tyne forms an inevitable skyline and the grounded brake van body is a pleasing touch. As is apparent in the earlier view, there is quite a deep cutting between this signal and the brake, yet it is less obvious in this view. The ladder up the post is rotting away and some of the rungs are broken. However, why is there so much of the battered old ladder on the ground, far more than was needed for the height of the post? Also, it appears that the photographer has tidied up the rickety old structure from the earlier view to make it a bit more presentable for a close-up. Photograph A.G. Forsyth, Initial Photographics.

Fine detail of the top of the post of signal No.2 at the approach to Tyne Dock's second fan of sidings. Its primitive lower quadrant arm is slotted into a recess in the post and the old woodwork, including the arm, could have dated from the establishment of the yards during the 1860s. A clear blue sky with a wisp of cloud formed the background on 23 March 1967. Photograph A.G. Forsyth, Initial Photographics.

A very tall North Eastern slotted-post home signal with a repeater also stood at the head of the second fan of sidings, controlling access from a different approach line. It bore the number 1 at its base. The repeater arm could well be a later addition as it is behind the post rather than in a slot. This time the ladder is in good condition, although the very steep climb would not be for the faint-hearted! In the background is a much shorter post associated with a link to the third fan of sidings. It has a flat pyramidal cap rather than a decorative finial or nothing in the case of the two slotted posts. The biscuit and cake works chimney peers over the embankment in this 23 March 1967 view. Photograph A.G. Forsyth, Initial Photographics.

Another fine North Eastern slotted post signal at Tyne Dock Yard on 23 March 1967. This one does have a slightly ornate, flat pyramidal cap, so maybe the others did originally. It was situated on a link between the throat of the third fan of sidings and higher level lines leading to the fourth fan. Refer back to the earlier panoramic views to see the relative position of these four signals. Approximately where the telegraph pole stands, this link crosses a short tunnel carrying low level lines to one of the loading gantries at the dock. Station Cottages and the Picture Palace cinema off Boldon Lane form the background, while behind these are the Stanhope & Tyne and Brandling Junction routes, Harton Junction and Tyne Dock station. Photograph A.G. Forsyth, Initial Photographics.

The prescribed nine loaded air-braked hoppers approach Tyne Dock Bank Top signal box behind D5109 and D5107 on 21 March 1967, the famous flow of imported iron ore bound for Consett's blast furnaces. Ten Derby Sulzer Type 2 diesels, D5102 to D5111, were based at Gateshead for these workings from late 1966 to the end of such traffic in 1974. These replaced Tyne Dock's celebrated BR Standard 9F 2-10-0s 92060-92066 and 92097-92099, which had hauled the trains since 1956. The imports, for many years from northern Spain, commenced in 1880. Banking was often required from Tyne Dock Bottom to Tyne Dock Bank Top and also in the hills of west Durham. T and T1 0-8-0s (LNER Q5) were used on these trains from 1901, T2s (LNER Q6) from 1913 and T3s (LNER Q7) from 1919. Tyne Dock Q7s, together with five O1 2-8-0s worked the traffic for many years, a characteristic feature being the compressed air pumps for operating doors on the hopper wagons. Photograph A.G. Forsyth, Initial Photographics.

The two BR Sulzer Type 2s were followed up the bank slightly later in the afternoon of 21 March 1967 by Q6 63366 on a very different freight working. This consists of a brake van and eleven goods vehicles comprising two wooden-bodied examples, six standard 16-ton mineral wagons, a couple of larger versions and one hopper. The engine was built in July 1913 at Darlington Works and was withdrawn from Tyne Dock in May 1967. Because of the importance and weight of the Consett ore traffic, the line was laid with well-maintained flat-bottom rail. This was probably the best track in the complex, although from these illustrations it will be seen that standards elsewhere in the yard were quite good. Photograph A.G. Forsyth, Initial Photographics.

Having deposited the bulk of its wagons from Tyne Dock Bottom, 63366 stands in the shadow of Tyne Dock Bank Top box with the 21-ton hopper and brake van from the rear of the train. This Q6 was one of a very small number which retained their original buffer beam consisting of wooden baulks sandwiched in steel plates. Although a newer design of buffer has been acquired, a different type of boiler with a more squat dome fitted and the cylinder lubricator moved from the top of the frame to the running plate, the appearance of the Q6 is essentially the same as when it was built. 63366 (as 1335) was only the 27th member of a class of 120 to be built. Photograph A.G. Forsyth, Initial Photographics.

During the morning, 63366 busied itself in the second fan of sidings at Tyne Dock Yard with a train of coal empties, the first three of which were hoppers. The fine water crane on the right was last seen on page 3. In its heyday, the layout at Tyne Dock Yard was very impressive. From west to east, beyond the tracks from Tyne Dock Bottom, the fans had sixteen, fourteen, thirteen and nine roads respectively. To the east of each fan were sunken tracks, in pairs or threes, leading to the gantries at the head of the dock. Even the approaches were on a large scale. There were thirteen tracks, including sidings, at Green Lane box and seventeen in line with Tyne Dock Bank Top box. Photograph A.G. Forsyth, Initial Photographics.

Q6 63366 now moves off from Tyne Dock Yard. During its BR days, the loco was always based in the Newcastle area. Throughout the 1950s it was at Borough Gardens, but by 1961 was at Blaydon and a further move took it to Tyne Dock by 1963. As mentioned earlier, it finished its days there a couple of months after these photographs were taken. The instructions to reach Tyne Dock shed from the beloved Ian Allan *Shed Directory* were as follows: *The shed is on the west side of a goods line known as the Pontop and South Shields branch. Turn left outside Tyne Dock station into Boldon Lane. Turn right into Green Lane, cross the railway bridge and turn right into a short dead-end. The shed is on the left side, 20 minutes walk from the station. Note - a circular bus service labelled 'Simonside' runs from the station to the corner of Green Lane.* Photograph A.G. Forsyth, Initial Photographics.

A final view of 63366 moving its empty hoppers out of the second fan of sidings at Tyne Dock Yard on 21 March 1967. The signal and retaining wall on the left can be seen in the earlier view of the signal with arms for both directions, thus helping to put the last few views in context. It is interesting to look at Tyne Dock's loco allocations at the beginning and end of the previous decade compared with the handful of withdrawn Q6s and stand-by K1s there in the last few weeks. In 1950 there were four Q6 and fifteen Q7 0-8-0s, four J25 0-6-0s, one G5 0-4-4T, two J71 and four J72 0-6-0Ts, two N8 and two N9 0-6-2Ts and nine WD Austerity 2-8-0s. In 1959 there were three Q6 and eleven Q7 0-8-0s, five O1 2-8-0s, one J21 and four J25 0-6-0s, two J71 and two J72 0-6-0Ts, two J94 0-6-0STs, two N10 0-6-2Ts, a T1 4-8-0T and ten 9F 2-10-0s. Photograph A.G. Forsyth, Initial Photographics.

This very interesting panorama looking north from Tyne Dock Bank Top box on 21 March 1967 shows the complete range of sidings mentioned earlier. They are described from left to right, together with the signals, which can be related to the relevant levers in the inside view of the box. Five general purpose sidings come first, two of which are visible. One of them is occupied by various open wagons, a tanker and a box van. A dinky little signal, No.11, controls access. Next comes 'Gantry', the incline up to the coal stage, the responsibility of signal No.12. Very unusually, the Tyne Dock coal stage was no less than 500 yards from the shed. To the right are the outward and inward engine lines, controlled by signal No.13. Finally, there are the 'Standage' sidings, one of which contains loaded coal wagons probably destined for the coal stage. Signal No.8, since demolished, was responsible for them and is represented by one of the white levers in the box. The other white levers were associated with closed sidings off the 'main line'. Signals 24 and 23 in the foreground controlled access from the five sidings to the shed yard and 'main line' respectively. To the left, a cutting is a reminder of the 1872 connection from the Jarrow line to Tyne Dock. In 1885 it was superseded by a more convenient line from St Bede's Junction further west. Particularly interesting in the distance (to the left of the giant pylon) is the ore loading bunker (long, low and dark) and beyond the pylon are the 'kangaroo' loading cranes. In between, white, is the bridge of a ship - so you begin to appreciate the climb up to Bank Top. Photograph A.G. Forsyth, Initial Photographics.

With the unmistakable coaling stage on the left, 63387 has a train of empty coal hoppers in the morning sunshine, on 23 March 1967. Along with 63344 and 63366, the engine retained its original North Eastern 'sandwich' buffer beam comprising timber planks between metal plates. The tender is a 4,125 gallon self-trimming type with curved coal rails at the rear. Other types of tender will be noticed on different engines. It was quite a well-travelled loco and belonged to several sheds during its lengthy career. Prior to the end of World War 2, few Q6s were allocated to Hartlepool but, as 2230, this particular engine was sent to Hartlepool East in January 1927 and was joined by three others. When East closed in 1939, its four Q6s moved to Hartlepool West, but had all gone by March 1943. In 1950 63387 was at Selby and from 1955 to 1959 at Tyne Dock, but by 1961 it had moved on to Blaydon, then Sunderland during 1963. It soon went to Neville Hill and in June 1966 was transferred to Normanton. This proved to be a short stay, as along with 63344, 63420 and 63426, it was transferred to Tyne Dock in October 1966. Photograph A.G. Forsyth, Initial Photographics.

Although Q6 63455 is in the familiar work-stained and somewhat rusting condition at Tyne Dock coaling stage around mid-day on 21March 1967, it does at least have its cylinder front casings in place, unlike many others of the class at the time. The shed plate has gone astray, but at least there is a shunting pole lodged above the front buffer beam. This engine was built at the nearby Armstrong Whitworth factory and delivered to the North Eastern in December 1920. After almost half a century of hard work it was withdrawn from Tyne Dock shed in June 1967. The brick base and timber superstructure of the coaler are apparent, the latter clearly having had some planks replaced in the recent past. Note the two substantial but redundant water cranes and the truncated remains of a third one above the rear of the tender, together with the two primitive coal chutes operated by chains. The one on the right was disused by this time. 63455 is on the engine outward road and a rather battered fire shovel lies between that and the inward road. Photograph A.G. Forsyth, Initial Photographics.

On 23 March 1967, J27 65817 has been coaled at Tyne Dock and has a full head of steam ready to resume its duties. As a pilot, the engine has a brake van in the typical North East tradition and the guard looks down at the driver who appears to be exasperated about something to do with the tender. The engine was built by North British Loco in May 1908 and has a tender with just two coal rails and 'D'-shaped openings in its frame. The loco itself has a short smokebox, a separate hand rail on the smokebox door, a medium-sized dome and a 'piano' front to the main frames. An original North Eastern composite front buffer beam survives, although this seems to have had a hefty shunting thump on its left side. Despite its woebegone appearance and the almost inevitable missing shed plate, the J27 is still a proud tribute to Edwardian design and engineering. 65817 was withdrawn in October 1964, but reinstated six days later, finally succumbing just before the end of steam at Tyne Dock in 1967. The inward engine line, headshunt and outward engine line are clearly displayed in this view. Photograph A.G. Forsyth, Initial Photographics.

K1 2-6-0 62025 in Tyne Dock shed yard on 21 March 1967 prior to making its way to the turntable. Prototype K1 3445 (familiar after Nationalisation as 61997 *MacCailin Mór*) was rebuilt from one of Gresley's 3-cylinder K4s by Thompson in 1945, to the latter's standard 2-cylinder arrangement. The production batch of 70, with modifications by Peppercorn, was ordered from North British Loco in 1947 and all entered service after the formation of British Railways. They proved almost as versatile as B1s and worked everything from fast passenger trains on the West Highland line to colliery trips in the North East. 62025 emerged from the North British Queens Park Works in Glasgow during August 1949. It was one of no less than fourteen delivered that month, the most prolific month during construction of the class, which took place between May 1949 and March 1950. It was originally a Blaydon engine, mainly for hauling 700 ton goods trains to Carlisle. From November 1962 until the shed closed in June 1966, 62025 was based at Alnmouth and was a frequent visitor to the grand little terminus at Alnwick on passenger trains. Its work-soiled demise from Tyne Dock in April 1967 was a matter of days after this photograph was taken. Photograph A.G. Forsyth, Initial Photographics.

It appears a casual task, almost, for the fireman of 62025, holding the vacuum 'on' for the outside turntable at Tyne Dock shed, near 'No.1' roundhouse, on the same day. This particular turntable was installed some time after 1890 and was 60ft in diameter. 'No.1' roundhouse itself had a 50ft turntable and two earlier roundhouses (see later for shed construction details) had 42ft turntables. The outside turning facilities at Tyne Dock were equipped for dealing with locos having vacuum brakes and the fireman of the K1 is taking advantage of this bit of technology. Otherwise, locos such as Q6s had to be shoved round manually, thus the footholds round the perimeter of the pit. Part of the art was to get the engine finely balanced on the turntable. The 1930s semis of Aldbrough Street form the background. Lightweight fencing separates back yards from railway property, a far cry from now! Photograph A.G. Forsyth, Initial Photographics.

Q6 63455 has its basic needs attended to over the ash pit outside Tyne Dock shed on Monday 19 June 1967. With the blower on, the final residue of accumulated debris is cleared out of the smokebox. There is plenty of ash encroaching on adjacent tracks and an old fire shovel, possibly discarded but maybe still of use on occasions. This view was taken just before the trip to the coal stage described opposite. During its BR career, 63455 was at Consett shed throughout the 1950s and early 1960s, before finishing its days on Tyneside. Hopefully, the lad with the shovel would soon escape from the grime for a nice mug of tea or a bottle of Newcastle Brown, whichever suited him! As mentioned in the introductory notes, an invaluable guide to the shed, its history and environs, is to be found in *A Tripe Supper with Leftover Monies* by Ian Sixsmith in *British Railways Illustrated* Vol. 16 number 9, June 2007. Photograph Paul Anderson.

On the afternoon of 19 June 1967, the author was fortunate to be invited into the cab of 63455 as it was serviced at the end of an arduous day hauling mineral wagons, as was the norm. The Q6 trundled off, from the coal stage to the shed. A few shovels of coal were aimed into the firebox to aid the movement and helped maintain light steam until the fire was built up the following morning. Point lever 16 and signal 14 would have been pulled off for this movement. The signal bridge at Bank Top, the 'economical' two-way signal at the approach to Tyne Dock Yard and the 1930s semi-detached houses in Hope Street, West Harton, are ahead. Photograph Paul Anderson.

No, you're not imagining this! Any visitor would have reeled in shock at the sight of these mighty A1 Pacifics, carefully tucked away in the Tyne Dock wagon repair shop next door to the roundhouses (there wasn't that much repair work going on by this late time, for the waning traffic made for an excess of wagons). The surprise would have been all the greater after the sorry fare of broken-down, rusty 0-6-0s and 0-8-0s in the yard outside. Jobs for Pacifics in the North East, even freight and coal, were disappearing and Tyne Dock, itself on its last legs, proved a handy and dry place to store a few, pending withdrawal or a return to traffic. There are five here, all apparently in good nick though without name plates of course – these would have been too vulnerable in the semi-deserted environs of Tyne Dock. On 25 April 1964 there are five here, all ex-Gateshead: 60116 HAL O' THE WYND, 60127 WILSON WORSDELL, 60129 GUY MANNERING, 60142 EDWARD FLETCHER and 60151 MIDLOTHIAN. Only two, GUY MANNERING and MIDLOTHIAN enjoyed a reprieve, going to York in June and July for a few months until withdrawal near the end of the year; they were in fact to be found working into Newcastle during that time. The other three were withdrawn in June 1965 and disposed of. Photograph A.G. Forsyth, Initial Photographics.

Most K1s at Tyne Dock were unkempt, although not quite as bad as this one. 62023, delivered from North British in August 1949, was withdrawn a matter of days after this photograph was taken on Wednesday 14 June 1967. Like 62025 seen earlier, this engine went new to Blaydon for Carlisle goods trains, but also worked passenger trains from Newcastle, to Blackhill, Consett and Hawick via both Hexham and Reedsmouth. It was also noted on race specials to Redcar. The loco was also at Alnmouth at the same time as 62025. During the early 1960s there was an increase in the use of K1s on relatively lowly trip workings to and from collieries in the North East, replacing withdrawn 0-6-0s. From 1964 they went to sheds that had not previously used them, such as Tyne Dock, although 62023 only spent its last year there. The poor old mogul is moving away to join Q6 63387 for the short run to the coal stage. Other K1s at Tyne Dock at the time were 62005, 62011, 62045, 62050 and 62060, the loco in the shed being one of the last four. Photograph Paul Anderson.

A fine portrait of Q6 63431 over the ash pit at Tyne Dock shed on the morning of 21 March 1967. Although work-stained like the rest, there has been an attempt to clean the BR emblem on the tender, the cabside number and the cast number plate on the smokebox door. Furthermore, the loco still has its shed plate. However, the boiler cladding does seem to be coming adrift behind the smokebox there and has been patched-up by the firebox. A shunting pole rests on the running plate above the buffer beam, which is the replacement single plate type. This is not the neatest part of the Tyne Dock complex and there are shovels and other assorted items of metalwork amid the piles of ash in the foreground. The houses of Aldbrough Street appear in the right background. 63431, as 2274, was at Newport shed on Tees-side in 1945. BR allocations included Selby in 1950, Borough Gardens during the latter half of the 1950s, Blaydon in 1961 and Tyne Dock by 1963. The loco had something of an adventure in June 1963 when it was in charge of a Stephenson Locomotive Society brake van tour of the Skinningrove area.Photograph A.G. Forsyth, Initial Photographics.

Now here *is* a sight; the Bank Top on 25 April 1965 and one of the local air-pump 9Fs, 92097, brings in a train of the special hoppers, the 8K08 14.50 working Tyne Dock to Consett. We often forget that there was also a sharp gradient up from the sea level of the dock and this had traditionally been banked too; you have to look hard but there, at the rear, is a diesel shunter serving as banker, successor to various 0-6-0s and 0-8-0s. What's remarkable is the fine condition of 92097, possibly recently dolled-up for an enthusiast job. It had returned from a Light Casual at Crewe a few weeks before, but it's hard to imagine Crewe cleaning it up for that. Photograph A.G. Forsyth, Initial Photographics.

That's more like it, situation normal and a 9F in proper 'BR grey-brown' tops the bank the next day, 26 April 1965. This is 92062 with ore for Consett and the usual diesel shunter follows up at the rear; heroically filthy, the 9F seems to be leaking steam all over the place. The situation at Tyne Dock was odd in that the shed's principal engines, the 2-10-0s, were too big to make use of the roundhouses, which after all formed the great part of the running shed; they could only be attended under cover in the straight shed. Photograph A.G. Forsyth, Initial Photographics.

A side view of Tyne Dock's smart K1 62005, contrasting with a decidedly grubby Q6 on 14 June 1967. The 0-8-0 conveniently masks the Derby Type 2s for the Consett ore traffic. Following delivery in June 1949, 62005 went to Darlington shed but was transferred to Heaton the following September. On 5 September 1950 it was observed working a braked goods from Doncaster to Kings Cross and returned on a parcels train from Palmers Green. It eventually moved back to Darlington and remained there until 1959 when it was sent to Ardsley to work holiday specials from Bradford Exchange to coastal resorts. In July of that year it was noted on a Cleethorpes train and reached Blackpool the following August Bank Holiday. It was at York for much of the 1960s before its sojourn at Tyne Dock. Photograph Paul Anderson.

It was not all decay, dereliction and rusty scrap, even this late in the day. On 25 April 1965 one of Tyne Dock's own Q6 0-8-0s, 63398 and a sight for sore eyes, eases into Bank Top with a mixed bag of hoppers and opens (including a couple of spare brakes in the middle) on 25 April 1965. Photograph A.G. Forsyth, Initial Photographics.

Despite their modest appearance, the J72 0-6-0Ts were remarkable little engines, not only in terms of power output, but also length of production and longevity. The first batch of twenty, to the design of Wilson Worsdell, emerged from Darlington Works in 1898-99. More followed from 1914 to 1922, bringing the total to 75 prior to Grouping in 1923. Another ten were built by the LNER at Doncaster during 1925 and a further 28 were constructed at Darlington from 1949 to 1951, after Nationalisation. They were allocated to sheds of all major constituents of the LNER, uniquely, and most carried on working until the 1960s. Tyne Dock had one of the first engines built and housed the last one to be withdrawn. That was Departmental No.58, seen here stored in the wagon repair shop alongside the main shed on 16 August 1967. As 69005, it had emerged from Darlington Works in November 1949 but was withdrawn from normal service during October 1964 and transferred to Departmental Stock, initially for de-freezing coal wagons on the shipping staithes at North Blyth. The tank only spent one winter on this duty before transfer to Gateshead in 1965, to provide steam for cleaning the bogies of diesel locos, unsuccessfully as it turned out. A spell de-icing points in Tyne Yard followed, but No.58 eventually went into store at Tyne Dock shed and was withdrawn in October 1967, to be sold for scrap in January 1968. Photograph A.G. Forsyth, Initial Photographics.

Q6 63429 poses against the grime, gunge, ash and flaking walls of 'No.1' roundhouse at Tyne Dock shed on 21 March 1967. This was the newest building but had its roof completely removed during 1960. Soon after building, it was felt necessary to provide a bit more room for larger engines. This materialised as four lean-to extensions with slate roofs and windows, two each in the south and west walls of the building. The tender of 63429 is partially in one of the latter. This particular engine was built locally by Armstrong Whitworth and delivered in May 1920. Throughout the 1950s it was allocated to Selby, but had moved to Blaydon by 1961 and Blyth by 1963. In earlier years, as 2272, it was a Hull Dairycoates engine. 63429 was withdrawn in July 1967 and no doubt the wonderful Victorian wheelbarrow in the foreground went the same way. Photograph A.G. Forsyth, Initial Photographics.

A study of the lower anatomy of 63429. Very probably, it could not have got much muckier than this. There are a few ash-encrusted wooden keys in the chairs on this particular shed road, but not many. The Q6 itself has had a heavy shunt at the front end, judging by the angle of the running plate behind the buffer beam. The cylinder casing is coming apart somewhat and all the motion is coated in oily grime, apart from the piston rod itself. The chalked measurements on the sand box presumably relate to some earlier valve setting work. The mechanical lubricator was originally on the frame in front of the second splasher but was moved to simplify the linkage. Photograph A.G. Forsyth, Initial Photographics.

No.63455 has already appeared in several earlier views, mucky but active. Here it is derelict and rusting at the back of Tyne Dock shed on 16 August 1967. The coupling rod has been removed from this side of the engine and both the shed plate and numberplate have gone. Weeds are springing up around the disused rails and even the venerable wheelbarrow has turned its clogs up. A similarly decaying Gresley coach, probably a redundant departmental vehicle by this date, languishes on the right. Although neglected, sad and awaiting cutting up, the Q6 still has a proud and dignified North Eastern appearance about it. When the author travelled on the footplate of this engine on 19 June 1967, it had a matter of days useful service ahead of it. Photograph A.G. Forsyth, Initial Photographics.

A melancholy scene at Tyne Dock shed on the afternoon of 16 August 1967. The derelict hulks of WD 2-8-0 90200 and J27 0-6-0 65860 await their inevitable fate in a barely discernible siding between the outside turntable (behind the camera) and the entrance to 'No.1' roundhouse (off to the right). 65860 was completed at Darlington Works in November 1921 and was withdrawn during May 1967. More details later. 90200, as War Department 7232, was on loan to the LNER from October 1943 to December 1944 when it was transferred to the Southern Railway. By March 1944, the LNER had no less than 350 Austerities on loan, Tyne Dock having about twenty of them at the time. This North British Hyde Park Works loco, as 77232, was again loaned to the LNER in March 1947 but finally managed to make it into BR ownership during 1948. During the 1950s and 1960s, 90200 had spells at York, Darlington, Low Moor, Sowerby Bridge and Sunderland before ending up in this ignominious state at Tyne Dock. Photograph A.G. Forsyth, Initial Photographics.

Q6 63395 inside the old Tyne Dock wagon repair shop on 9 August 1968 was undoubtedly the celebrity of the class. The engine was turned out by Darlington in December 1918 as 2238, the 56th of a class of 120. Although the first thirty T2s were built in 1913, the war delayed construction and no more were built during 1914-16. Production resumed in April 1917 and finished in March 1921, Armstrong Whitworth of Newcastle being responsible for the construction of 50 of them from November 1919. In fact that company turned out no less than seven in February 1920. 63395 spent nearly all of the 1950s at Selby shed, but was transferred to Darlington in June 1959 for goods workings between Croft Yard and Consett via Ferryhill and Lanchester. On one occasion it was derailed just south of Consett and ended up on its side. The loco went to Sunderland during the mid-1960s and was withdrawn from there in September 1967. After narrowly avoiding being scrapped, 63395 was purchased by the North Eastern Locomotive Preservation Society and began operating on the North Yorkshire Moors Railway in June 1970. Probably its proudest moment was taking part in the Stockton & Darlington 150th anniversary procession during 1975. Photograph A.G. Forsyth, Initial Photographics.

Moving north from Tyne Dock to the Northumberland side of the river, the lines around Blyth, some twelve miles north of Newcastle, saw plenty of BR steam during the 1960s. Ivatt 4MT 43123 presents a functional rather than handsome appearance on 22 March 1967 as it grinds tender first round the curve between Winning Junction and Marchey's House Junction 1¾ miles north-west of Cambois. The spoil heaps of abandoned West Sleekburn colliery form the skyline to the right, while smoke from the loco drifts over ground leading down to the River Wansbeck on the left. 43123 was built at Horwich in August 1951 and its withdrawal from Blyth came in July 1967. In between it spent the bulk of the 1950s at Selby before moving to Hull Dairycoates, then West Hartlepool and finally Blyth. Photograph A.G. Forsyth, Initial Photographics.

West Sleekburn Junction, on the Blyth & Tyne line about ten miles north of Newcastle, on the afternoon of 23 March 1967. The curve beyond the box leads to Winning Junction, actually at West Sleekburn village, then North Blyth and Cambois. The Marchey's House-Winning curve forming the third side of the triangle is this side of the distant houses. Branches to abandoned collieries at Bomarsund and West Sleekburn went off to the left of the cabin and alongside the hedge on the far right respectively. Within three months there were two devastating events here. In August 1959 fire destroyed the original North Eastern signal box, but towards the end of the year it was replaced by the BR (North Eastern Region) Type 17 cabin seen here. The old box was off to the right on the other side of the tracks. Meanwhile, with a temporary Block Cabin in position, there was a tragic accident involving two coal trains at 7.22pm on 4 November 1959. One train was to be held at West Sleekburn's up main home signal, seen here just to the right of the new box, but the driver of the J27 could not hold the train despite its low speed. The gradient approaching the signal had been distorted by mining subsidence. The train drifted into the path of another coal train running at about 30mph under clear signals onto the Cambois branch. A head-on collision occurred and the driver and fireman of the down train were killed instantly. Their engine, J27 65824, was subsequently written off. Photograph A.G. Forsyth, Initial Photographics.

Marchey's House Junction looking north towards Ashington and Newbiggin on 22 March 1967, with the line from Winning Junction and North Blyth coming in from the right. Does anyone know who Marchey was and what was special about his house? The Junction box is a North Eastern N2 type dating from 1895. The Blyth & Tyne opened between the two rivers in its title during 1846, utilising earlier wagonways for some of its course. An extension from Newsham to Bedlington followed during 1850 and the railway between Bedlington and North Seaton was authorised in 1857. That is the 'main line' seen in this and the previous view. Coal shipments from Cambois, on the north bank of the River Blyth, began in 1867 and the branch from West Sleekburn opened the same year. The North Eastern took over the Blyth & Tyne in 1874 and by 1890 coal shipments from Blyth reached 1¾ million tons a year. During 1893 the curve from Marchey's House to Winning was authorised allowing, at last, a direct route from the very productive Ashington pits to the staithes. Photograph A.G. Forsyth, Initial Photographics.

J27 65811 takes the West Sleekburn route at Winning Junction with a train of empty hoppers on 22 March 1967. The engine was built by North British in May 1908 and was one of the very last to be withdrawn, in September 1967. There were detail differences within the class; in this case note the large dome, three-rail tender and single plate buffer beam. The village of West Sleekburn is just off to the right and the minor road over the crossing connects Stakeford near Ashington with East Sleekburn and Cambois. Houses in the left distance, on the far side of the River Wansbeck, make up the village of North Seaton Colliery, while the caravans just visible above the wagons overlook the Wansbeck estuary and the North Sea. Photograph A.G. Forsyth, Initial Photographics.

On 22 March 1967 J27 65860 veers north on the spur from Winning Junction to Marchey's House Junction with empties for one of the collieries in the Ashington area. Variations from 65811 opposite are a squat dome, two-rail tender and composite wood/metal buffer beam. For part of the 1950s, 65860 was a bit of a wanderer, being allocated to Stockton in 1950, Newport in 1955 and Darlington in 1957. It was at Percy Main in 1963 and Blyth by 1966. The tidal lower reaches of the River Wansbeck, amounting to three miles, passed the mining communities of Guide Post, Sheepwash (names obviously dating from more bucolic times) then Stakeford, Ashington, West Sleekburn and North Seaton Colliery. This was quite a contrast to the river's origin some twenty miles to the west at Plashetts, 750ft up in the fells, and its passage across Northumberland through Kirkwhelpington, Meldon Park, Milford and Morpeth. Photograph A.G. Forsyth, Initial Photographics.

Slightly earlier in the day, J27 65811 heads towards Marchey's House Junction and the Ashington area with a brake van, probably to collect a train of coal for Cambois Power Station. Winning box has returned the home signal to its horizontal position very promptly. Permanent way details are interesting in this view. There are a few concrete sleepers lying around, yet no evidence of them on the actual running lines. Bullhead rail is the norm, except for some of the track from Marchey's House Junction which had been re-laid with flat bottom rail. A touch of fresh stone ballast had been laid on the up line at West Sleekburn Junction, but elsewhere ash ballast seems to suffice. Photograph A.G. Forsyth, Initial Photographics.

K1 62057 storms towards West Sleekburn Junction with a short rake of empty coal hoppers and a couple of brake vans on 22 March 1967, leaving a trail of smoke around Winning box. The engine was completed at the North British Queens Park Works in November 1949, one of seven turned out that month, and was destined to have some interesting adventures before withdrawal in May 1967. Initially it was based in the North East, at Darlington during 1950 then Haverton Hill in 1955. The engine had migrated to York by 1957 and was still there in 1965, but Blyth was its home by November 1966. York engines tended to stray from their normal duties and 62057 was no exception. On 1 August 1957 the loco was observed passing Gerrards Cross on the GW/GC Joint line with an empty rake of Southern Region passenger stock, while on 16 September 1957 it left Sheffield Victoria with 73005 on a Cardiff-Newcastle express. On 30 January 1959 it was yard pilot at Yaxley, about the last use of K1s on the GN main line. During 1965 it explored the country on goods trains, including Birmingham Washwood Heath-Cardiff and York-Bristol workings. Photograph A.G. Forsyth, Initial Photographics.

Ivatt 2-6-0 43123 hauls a train of loaded coal hoppers round the curve from Marchey's House Junction to Winning Junction on the sunny afternoon of 22 March 1967. Marchey's House box is just behind the semi-detached houses in the background. Even further away, just to the right of the engine, is the spoil heap of Ashington Colliery. This is probably another working from one of the Ashington area pits to Cambois Power Station. Photograph A.G. Forsyth, Initial Photographics.

More coal on its way from Ashington to Cambois, on 22 March 1967. Again, Marchey's House Junction is to the right and the houses on the left are part of the ribbon development alongside the secondary road between Stakeford and Bedlington Station. Unlike many of its wandering brethren, 65811 was allocated to Blyth from wartime to its demise in 1967. The driver beams down at the photographer from his cab. This March day was fairly benign, but in harsh winter conditions tender-first running was very unpopular with crews. Sheeting, which could be rolled down from the cab roof, is visible in this view and elsewhere. The three-rail tender with D-shaped openings in the frames is well shown. Photograph A.G. Forsyth, Initial Photographics.

65885 heads yet more coal from Ashington pit to Cambois on 22 March 1967. This was the first of the batch of ten ordered from Darlington Works on 14 December 1922, just over a fortnight before the North Eastern Railway ceased to exist, and entered service with the LNER in June 1923 as No. 2383. It was built as a superheated loco, like all of the post World War 1 examples, but in July 1943 became the first to be converted to saturated steam like the bulk of the class. The engine seems to be shedding a prolific amount of steam from its inside cylinders as it grinds round the Marchey's House Junction - Winning Junction curve, but managed to survive until June 1967. 65885 had a varied BR career, being allocated to Leeds Neville Hill in 1948, York during the early 1950s, Selby in the mid to late 1950s, York again by 1961 and Sunderland in 1963. It obviously ended its days at Blyth. Photograph A.G. Forsyth, Initial Photographics.

Ivatt 4MT 2-6-0 43055 rounds the curve from West Sleekburn Junction to Winning Junction with ten loaded hoppers and a couple of brake vans on the morning of 22 March 1967. The coal was probably from one of the pits in the Bedlington area and the two brakes suggest a reversal. The engine was completed at Darlington Works in September 1950 and withdrawn from Blyth during July 1967. It certainly moved around, being at Darlington in 1950, Kirkby Stephen in 1955, Heaton in 1957, Leeds Holbeck in 1959 and York in 1961. North Blyth shed was the preserve of a few Ivatt 4MTs towards the end, but South Blyth housed a few J27s when it closed to steam in May 1967. The allocation of the combined depots was very different back in 1950, comprising two J21 and 24 J27 0-6-0s, six G5 0-4-4Ts for passenger work and seven J77 0-6-0Ts. Even the telegraph poles hereabouts suffered from subsiding ground. Photograph A.G. Forsyth, Initial Photographics.

43055 on the West Sleekburn Junction-Winning Junction curve, again on 22 March 1967, but this time tender first. The colliery in the background of these views is at Bomarsund and the terraced cottages are on the edge of Stakeford. Track maintenance is indifferent, with a number of chair keys missing and ash ballast absent from sleeper ends in the foreground. Allocations at the two Blyth sheds in 1959 was very straightforward. Apart from two J25 0-6-0s a J77 0-6-0T and seven diesel shunters, there was a hefty total of thirty J27 0-6-0s for mineral work. Photograph A.G. Forsyth, Initial Photographics.

A long train of hoppers is hauled round the West Sleekburn Junction-Winning Junction spur by South Blyth 65855 on 23 March 1967. The engine was built by Beyer Peacock of Manchester and entered service as North Eastern No. 1226 in August 1908. Delivery of the 115 North Eastern P3s commenced in April 1906 with No. 790 (BR 65780) and finished in September 1923 when No. 2392 (BR 65894) was completed. During early LNER days, over half the class were based at four sheds - Percy Main, Newport, Shildon and Sunderland. However, odd ones found employment at places as diverse as Carlisle, Tweedmouth and Hull. By 1935, Whitby on the coast and Waskerley high on the moors above Weardale had one each. South Blyth had also acquired its first J27 by this time, the two Blyth sheds having no less than 19 of them by 1943. 65855 was at Haverton Hill then Thornaby from Nationalisation to the 1960s but was withdrawn from Blyth in September 1967. Photograph A.G. Forsyth, Initial Photographics.

The West Sleekburn-Winning curve again, with 65811 leading a short and varied train of mineral wagons on 23 March 1967. Rather surprisingly, forty years later the landscape in this area had not changed that much. The former Blyth & Tyne route serving Morpeth, Lynemouth aluminium smelter and Blyth docks was intact and there was still plenty of open countryside around West Sleekburn, Marchey's House and Winning Junctions. At Winning Junction level crossing the colliery tip had been landscaped, the row of miners' terraces had been demolished and the site of the mine itself was occupied by an industrial estate. The main part of West Sleekburn was much the same, and one row of terraces bore the name 'Marshes Houses' - perhaps the origin of 'Marchey's House'? Much of the Ashington Colliery site had been landscaped and part of it was occupied by Wansbeck Business Park. Almost inevitably, a major road had been thrust across the railway between Winning and Cambois. This was the A189 between Cramlington north of Newcastle and Ellington near Morpeth, serving Blyth and Newbiggin on the way. Photograph A.G. Forsyth, Initial Photographics.

South Blyth shed on 22 March 1967, with three J27s in residence. The one on the left is in steam but that in the middle has a 'not to be moved' indicator on it. Neither can be identified. To the right is 65861, finished by Darlington Works in December 1921 and withdrawn in May 1967. Allocations included York in 1950, Selby during the late 1950s and Blyth by the early 1960s. The 1947 *Shed Directory* instructions for South Blyth (the station closed in 1964) were as follows: *The shed is on the north side of the line, west of the station. Turn right outside the station, right along Delavel Terrace, then right into Morpeth Road. The shed entrance is on the right just after the level crossing. Walking time 5 minutes.* The directions for North Blyth were a lot more interesting: *The shed is in dockland on the north bank of the river. There is no passenger service to North Blyth. Turn right outside Blyth station into Turner Street, continue into Regent Street. Turn left into Hodgsons Lane, right almost immediately into Crawford Street and right into Ferry Street. Cross on the ferry. Turn right at the north end of the ferry, follow the road round to the left under a railway bridge. The shed entrance is on the left.* Photograph A.G. Forsyth, Initial Photographics.

West Hartlepool shed on 17 August 1967, less than three weeks before it closed. Two WD 2-8-0s and a K1 are visible. 90076 started life as War Department 77276 and was built by North British in August 1944. The loco was on loan to the LNER from November 1945 and was purchased by the company during December 1946. It was classified O7 in January 1947 and became 63076 in July 1948 until BR renumbered it 90076 during July 1950. Allocated to Newport until 1959, it was transferred to Wakefield and finally West Hartlepool. It was one of the last to be withdrawn, in September 1967. Note the state of the track this side of the K1 tender! The NER sheds, as a breed, were amongst the oldest in the land and were seldom updated. Accordingly they developed into an eccentric range of sites and buildings; this three road shed, for instance, sat some distance to the north of the main shed, a cramped double roundhouse close by Newburn Bridge - see opposite. Keep an eye out for the ongoing series on NER Sheds in *British Railways Illustrated*, the monthly magazine published by Irwell Press. Photograph A.G. Forsyth, Initial Photographics.

West Hartlepool shed on 17 August 1967, at 5.15pm if the clock is correct. The first building is 'No.1' roundhouse with 50ft turntable; behind was 'No.2' still with only a 42ft table. On the right, poor old 63431 has had its coupling rods removed and has trapped a despairing wooden-bodied mineral wagon which seems to have shed its load. Similarly abandoned 63397 holds a record for the class. The engine was built at Darlington in December 1918 and no doubt went about its duties locally in the North East until it had a bit of an adventure on 16 October 1945. Based at Newport shed at the time, the loco was observed at Ferme Park on the GN main line between Hornsey and Harringay in north London. This is almost certainly the furthest south a Q6 strayed. After this it settled down at West Hartlepool until withdrawn in May 1967. Note the detail differences in the tenders, longer coal rails and D-shaped frame openings for 63431 and shorter coal rails and oval frame openings for 63397. Photograph A.G. Forsyth, Initial Photographics.

Four mineral wagons, a wooden cabin and a bike overlook 90360 at West Hartlepool shed coaling stage on 17 August 1967. The engine was built by North British as War Department 77296 in September 1944. A total of 935 were built by North British and Vulcan Foundry from 1943 to 1945. All but three went overseas and most of them returned to Britain. From 1949 to 1951 this particular one was at Redhill shed on the Southern before making its way to the North East via Newton Heath (1955), Sowerby Bridge (1957) and Wakefield (1963 - including a period of store there during 1967). The chalk scrawl on the tender is WHOS SORRY NOW, the title of a popular song but no doubt lamenting the demise of BR steam in the North East. For more WD finery see Irwell's latest offering, The Book of the WD 2-8-0s and 2-10-0s. Photograph A.G. Forsyth, Initial Photographics.

Tyne Dock's 'No.1' roundhouse, open to the elements, on 25 April 1965. The authorities at least saw fit to put a form of shelter around the shear legs but with the occupant, Q6 63371 in steam, it has probably been abandoned for lifting purposes by now. 63368, 63411 and 63453 are the other Q6s, gathered round in time-honoured fashion. During 1858, before the opening of Tyne Dock itself in March 1859, an engine shed was authorised about half a mile south of the basin and alongside the former Pontop & South Shields and Brandling Junction routes. It opened in 1862, maybe a bit earlier, and was described as a 'round shed', although apparently no plan of it has been discovered. As a result of a huge increase in mineral traffic, the original shed was replaced by a row of three square buildings from 1870 to 1878, approximately. The southernmost two, nearest Green Lane, were 'square roundhouses' with 42ft turntables and the other one may well have been the same at first, although it had certainly been refashioned into the straight shed by 1880. By about 1890 another square roundhouse with a 50ft turntable had appeared on the west side – this was 'No.1'. At Grouping in 1923 Tyne Dock had an allocation of 94 engines. At Nationalisation in 1948 BR designated the shed 54B in the Sunderland District and the allocation was 59. In September 1958 it became 52H under Newcastle when the Sunderland District was abolished; closure came on 9 September 1967. The site is now a housing development. Photograph A.G. Forsyth, Initial Photographics.

South Dock shed at Sunderland on 17 August 1967. At Grouping in 1923 it had an allocation of 88; at nationalisation in 1948, it became 54A and had 58 locos. It was recoded 52G in the Newcastle district when the Sunderland district was abolished in September 1958. To the left is WD 2-8-0 90348, withdrawn in September 1967 when the shed closed. I missed a tremendous opportunity on Saturday 24 June 1967, rued ever since. During the previous evening , while on the footplate of a WD, the driver had invited me to travel with him the next day to Consett. I was forced to decline as I had to travel back from Durham University to Leicester the next day. How I wish I'd stayed that extra day! Photograph A.G. Forsyth, Initial Photographics.

The celebrity at Sunderland was J27 65894, seen here on 17 August 1967. Clearly it was well looked after. As 2392 it emerged from Darlington Works in September 1923, one of ten ordered by the North Eastern in December 1922 on the very eve of Grouping and delivered to the LNER. It proved to be the last of the class of 115 engines which served the North East admirably for over 60 years. In this view, the large boiler and generous cab of 65894 contrasts with the rather small tender, albeit piled high for the duties ahead. The loco went new to Darlington shed but soon moved to Ferryhill to cover Durham coalfield workings. In 1930 it was transferred to York for local goods workings to Scarborough and remained there until October 1966 when a final transfer took it to Sunderland. On 9 September it worked the last diagrammed steam turn from that shed. Following withdrawal, 65894 was purchased for preservation and started work on the North Yorkshire Moors Railway in October 1971. Photograph A.G. Forsyth, Initial Photographics.

Evening comes at Bank Top and 92060 glides by on 25 April 1965, its day done. The diesels were well in charge by now, though the Consett jobs demonstrated some of the shortcomings of the new traction. The 9Fs covered at times, but the Type 2s in tandem were working most of the iron ore trains while a Tyne Yard English Electric Type 4 had taken over the South Pelaw-Consett banking. The irony was that while the diesels indeed enjoyed better (but not strikingly better) availability they could not do more 'work' than the Tyne Dock 9Fs; there were only so many trips a day and that was that. Moreover, BR was now using two locomotives, thus doubling the maintenance requirements, for jobs previously performed by a single 2-10-0. As for the EE Type 4, while mileage/availability figures might (or might not!) be truly wondrous up and down the East Coast main line, to have it sitting there performing a few banking jobs every day was a spectacular waste of money. Photograph A.G. Forsyth, Initial Photographics.

A last look at Tyne Dock and No.92061, one of the ten 9Fs specially fitted with air pumps for the working of the Consett ore trains. The initial batch of seven, 92060-92066, worked on the Midland at first, replacing poor-performing Crosti 2-8-0s at Wellingborough. In 1955, though readied for the pumps and the associated fittings (cut-outs were made in the running plate and so on) the pumps were not actually fixed until the following year. The 9Fs stopped off at Crewe for the work to be done and then made their way to what was to be their long home at Tyne Dock in 1956. They were followed by 92097-92099. The air pumps were there to activate the discharge doors on the special hopper wagons. There were two, at about 90lb/in^2 pressure. One served to keep the four side discharge doors on each wagon shut when loading and running (there was also a manual safety device) and the other opened the doors to discharge the ore onto the conveyor at Consett, which led to the furnaces. It was a hard life and 92061 has an understandably weary look about it in the yard at Tyne Dock shed. Photograph A.G. Forsyth, Initial Photographics.

A little to the south of Tyne Dock the Gateshead-Sunderland line met the line up to Consett on the level at Pontop Crossing. On 12 June 1964 Q6 63436 rubbles past PONTOP XING box, as its board proclaims, heading east in the Sunderland direction; the Consett route of the iron ore trains runs south to north left to right under its wheels. Photograph A.G. Forsyth, Initial Photographics.